THE HABIT DOES NOT MAKE THE MONK

G. F. WATTS

BY

G. K. CHESTERTON

AUTHOR OF "ROBERT BROWNING," ETC.

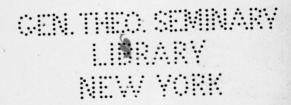
1906

LONDON DUCKWORTH & CO.

NEW YORK: E. P. DUTTON & CO.

Published 1904
Reprinted 1906

TURNBULL AND SPEARS, PRINTERS, EDINBURGH.

LIST OF ILLUSTRATIONS

LIST OF ILLUSTRATIONS

The Illustrations are from photographs by Fredk. Hollyer.

GEORGE FREDERICK WATTS was born on 23rd February 1817, and is still alive.* His whole rise and career, that is to say, synchronises roughly with the rise and career of the nineteenth century. As a rule, no doubt such chronological parallels are peculiarly fanciful and unmeaning. Nothing can be imagined more idle, in a general way, than talking about a century as if it were some kind of animal with a head and tail, instead of an arbitrary length cut from an unending scroll. Nor is it less erroneous to assume that even if a period be definitely vital or disturbing, art must be a mirror of it ; the greatest political storm flutters only a fringe of humanity ; poets, like brick-layers, work on through a century of wars, and Bewick's birds, to take an instance, have the air of persons unaffected by the French Revolution. But in the case of Watts there are two circumstances which render the dates relevant. The first is that the nineteenth

* He died on 1st July 1904.

century was self-conscious, believed itself to
be an idea and an atmosphere, and changed its
name from a chronological almost to a philosophical term. I do not know whether all
centuries do this or whether an advanced and
progressive organ called "The Eleventh Century" was ever in contemplation in the dawn
of the Middle Ages. But with us it is clear
that a certain spirit was rightly or wrongly
associated with the late century and that it
called up images and thoughts like any historic
or ritual date, like the Fourth of July or the
First of April. What these images and
thoughts were we shall be obliged in a few
minutes and in the interests of the subject to
enquire. But this is the first circumstance
which renders the period important; and the
second is that it has always been so regarded
by Watts himself. He more than any other
modern man, more than politicians who
thundered on platforms or financiers who
captured continents, has sought in the midst
of his quiet and hidden life to mirror his age.
He was born in the white and austere dawn
of that great reforming century, and he has
lingered after its grey and doubtful close. He

is above all things a typical figure, a survival
of the nineteenth century.

It will appear to many a somewhat grotesque
matter to talk about a period in which most of
us were born and which has only been dead a
year or two, as if it were a primal Babylonian
empire of which only a few columns are left
crumbling in the desert. And yet such is, in
spirit, the fact. There is no more remarkable
psychological element in history than the way
in which a period can suddenly become unin-
telligible. To the early Victorian period we
have in a moment lost the key : the Crystal
Palace is the temple of a forgotten creed.
The thing always happens sharply : a whisper
runs through the salons, Mr Max Beerbohm
waves a wand and a whole generation of great
men and great achievement suddenly looks mil-
dewed and unmeaning. We see precisely the
same thing in that other great reaction towards
art and the vanities, the Restoration of Charles
II. In that hour both the great schools of faith
and valour which had seemed either angels or
devils to all men : the dreams of Strafford and
the great High Churchmen on the one hand ;
the Moslem frenzy of the English Commons,

the worship of the English law upon the other; both seemed distant and ridiculous. The new Cavalier despised the old Cavalier even more than he despised the Roundhead. The last stand of English chivalry dwindled sharply to the solitary figure of the absurd old country gentleman drinking wine out of an absurd old flagon. The great roar of Roundhead psalms which cried out that the God of Battles was loose in English meadows shrank to a single snuffle. The new and polite age saw the old and serious one exactly as we see the early Victorian era: they saw it, that is to say, not as splendid, not as disastrous, not as fruitful, not as infamous, not as good or bad, but simply as ugly. Just as we can see nothing about Lord Shaftesbury but his hat, they could see nothing about Cromwell but his nose. There is no doubt of the shock and sharpness of the silent transition. The only difference is that accordingly as we think of man and his nature, according to our deepest intuitions about things, we shall see in the Restoration and the *fin de siècle* philosophy a man waking from a turbid and pompous dream, or a man hurled from heaven and the wars of the angels.

4

G. F. WATTS, R.A.

Photograph from life by Frederick Hollyer]

GEORGE FREDERICK WATTS

G. F. Watts is so deeply committed to, and so unalterably steeped in this early Victorian seriousness and air of dealing with great matters, that unless we sharply apprehend that spirit, and its difference from our own, we shall misunderstand his work from the outset. Splendid as is the art of Watts technically or obviously considered, we shall yet find much in it to perplex and betray us, unless we understand his original theory and intention, a theory and intention dyed deeply with the colours of a great period which is gone. The great technical inequalities of his work, its bursts of stupendous simplicity in colour and design, its daring failures, its strange symbolical portraits, all will mislead or bewilder if we have not the thread of intention. In order to hold that, we must hold something which runs through and supports, as a string supports jewels, all the wars and treaties and reforms of the nineteenth century.

There are at least three essential and preliminary points on which Watts is so completely at one with the nineteenth century and so completely out of accord with the twentieth, that it may be advisable to state them briefly before we proceed to the narrower but not more cogent facts of his life and growth. The first of these is a nineteenth century atmosphere which is so difficult to describe, that we can only convey it by a sort of paradox. It is difficult to know whether it should be called doubt or faith. For if, on the one hand, real faith would have been more confident, real doubt, on the other hand, would have been more indifferent. The attitude of that age of which the middle and best part of Watts' work is most typical, was an attitude of devouring and concentrated interest in things which were by their own system, impossible or unknowable. Men were, in the main, agnostics: they said, " We do not know "; but not one of them ever ventured to say, " We do not care." In most eras of revolt and question, the sceptics reap something from their scepticism: if a man were a believer in the eighteenth century, there was Heaven; if he were an unbeliever, there was the Hell-Fire Club. But these men restrained themselves more than hermits for a hope that was more than half hopeless, and sacrificed hope itself for a liberty which they would not enjoy; they were rebels without deliverance and saints without reward.

8

THE RIDER ON THE WHITE HORSE

There may have been and there was something arid and over-pompous about them: a newer and gayer philosophy may be passing before us and changing many things for the better; but we shall not easily see any nobler race of men, and of them all most assuredly there was none nobler than Watts. If anyone wishes to see that spirit, he will see it in pictures painted by Watts in a form beyond expression sad and splendid. *Hope* that is dim and delicate and yet immortal, the indestructible minimum of the spirit; *Love and Death* that is awful and yet the reverse of horrible; *The Court of Death* that is like a page of Epictetus and might have been dreamt by a dead Stoic: these are the visions of that spirit and the incarnations of that time. Its faith was doubtful, but its doubt was faithful. And its supreme and acute difference from most periods of scepticism, from the later Renascence, from the Restoration and from the hedonism of our own time was this, that when the creeds crumbled and the gods seemed to break up and vanish, it did not fall back, as we do, on things yet more solid and definite, upon art and wine and high finance and industrial efficiency and vices. It fell in love with abstractions and became enamoured of great and desolate words.

The second point of *rapport* between Watts and his time was a more personal matter, a matter more concerned with the man, or at least, the type; but it throws so much light upon almost every step of his career that it may with advantage be suggested here. Those who know the man himself, the quaint and courtly old man who is still living down at Limnerslease, know that if he has one trait more arresting than another, it is his almost absurd humility. He even disparages his own talent that he may insist rather upon his aims. His speech and gesture are simple, his manner polite to the point of being deprecating, his soul to all appearance of an almost confounding clarity and innocence. But although these appearances accurately represent the truth about him, though he is in reality modest and even fantastically modest, there is another element in him, an element which was in almost all the great men of his time, and it is something which many in these days would call a kind of splendid and inspired impudence. It is that wonderful if simple power of preach-

ing, of claiming to be heard, of believing in
an internal message and destiny: it is the
audacious faculty of mounting a pulpit. Those
would be very greatly mistaken, who, misled
by the child-like and humble manner of this
monk of art, expected to find in him any
sort of doubt, or any sort of fear, or any
sort of modesty about the aims he follows or
the cause he loves. He has the one great
certainty which marks off all the great Victorians from those who have come after them :
he may not be certain that he is successful, or
certain that he is great, or certain that he is
good, or certain that he is capable : but he is
certain that he is right. It is of course the
very element of confidence which has in our
day become least common and least possible.
We know we are brilliant and distinguished,
but we do not know we are right. We swagger
in fantastic artistic costumes ; we praise ourselves ; we fling epigrams right and left ; we
have the courage to play the egoist and the
courage to play the fool, but we have not the
courage to preach. If we are to deliver a
philosophy it must be in the manner of the
late Mr Whistler and the *ridentem dicere verum*,

GEORGE FREDERICK WATTS

If our heart is to be aimed at it must be with the rapier of Stevenson which runs us through without either pain or puncture. It is only just to say, that good elements as well as bad ones have joined in making this old Victorian preaching difficult or alien to us. Humility as well as fear, camaraderie as well as cynicism, a sense of complexity and a kind of gay and worldly charity have led us to avoid the pose of the preacher, to be moral by ironies, to whisper a word and glide away. But, whatever may be the accidental advantage of this recoil from the didactic, it certainly does mean some loss of courage and of the old and athletic simplicity. Nay, in some sense it is really a loss of a fine pride and self-regard. Mr Whistler coquetted and bargained about the position and sale of his pictures: he praised them; he set huge prices on them; but still under all disguise, he treated them as trifles. Watts, when scarcely more than a boy and comparatively unknown, started his great custom of offering his pictures as gifts worthy of a great nation. Thus we come to the conclusion, a conclusion which may seem to some to contain a faint element of paradox, that Mr Whistler suffered from an

LESLIE STEPHEN

excessive and exaggerated modesty. And this unnatural modesty of Mr Whistler can scarcely be more typically symbolised than in his horror of preaching. The new school of art and thought does indeed wear an air of audacity, and breaks out everywhere into blasphemies, as if it required any courage to say a blasphemy. There is only one thing that it requires real courage to say, and that is a truism.

Lastly, it would be quite impossible to complete this prefatory suggestion of the atmosphere in which the mind of Watts grew and prevailed, without saying something about that weary and weather-beaten question of the relation of art to ethics on which so much has been said in connection with him and his contemporaries. About the real aim and the real value of Watts' allegorical pictures I shall speak later, but for the moment it is only desirable to point out what the early and middle Victorian view of the matter really was. According to the later æsthetic creed which Mr Whistler and others did so much to preach, the state of the arts under the reign of that Victorian view was a chaos of everyone minding everyone else's business.

It was a world in which painters were trying
to be novelists, and novelists trying to be
historians, and musicians doing the work of
schoolmasters, and sculptors doing the work of
curates. That is a view which has some truth
in it, both as a description of the actual state of
things and as involving an interesting and suggestive philosophy of the arts. But a good deal
of harm may be done by ceaselessly repeating to
ourselves even a true and fascinating fashionable
theory, and a great deal of good by endeavouring to realise the real truth about an older
one. The thing from which England suffers
just now more than from any other evil is not
the assertion of falsehoods, but the endless
and irrepressible repetition of half-truths.
There is another side to every historic situation,
and that often a startling one; and the other
side of the Victorian view of art, now so out
of mode, is too little considered. The salient
and essential characteristic of Watts and men of
his school was that they regarded life as a
whole. They had in their heads, as it were,
a synthetic philosophy which put everything
into a certain relation with God and the
wheel of things. Thus, psychologically speak-

WALTER CRANE

ing they were incapable not merely of holding
such an opinion, but actually of thinking such
a thought as that of art for art's sake; it was
to them like talking about voting for voting's
sake, or amputating for amputating's sake.
To them as to the ancient Jews the Spirit of
the unity of existence declared in thunder
that they should not make any graven image,
or have any gods but He.   Doubtless, they
did not give art a relation of unimpeachable
correctness: in their scheme of things it may
be true, or rather it is true, that the æsthetic
was confused with the utilitarian, that good
gardens were turned so to speak into bad
cornfields, and a valuable temple into a useless
post-office.   But in so far as they had this
fundamental idea that art must be linked to
life, and to the strength and honour of nations,
they were a hundred times more broad-minded
and more right than the new ultra-technical
school.   The idea of following art through
everything for itself alone, through extravagance, through cruelty, through morbidity, is
just exactly as superstitious as the idea of
following theology for itself alone through
extravagance and cruelty and morbidity.   To

deny that Baudelaire is loathsome, or Nietzsche inhuman, because we stand in awe of beauty, is just the same thing as denying that the Court of Pope Julius was loathsome, or the rack inhuman, because we stand in awe of religion. It is not necessary and it is not honest. The young critics of the Green Carnation, with their nuances and technical mysteries, would doubtless be surprised to learn that as a class they resemble ecstatic nuns, but their principle is, in reality, the same. There is a great deal to be said for them, and a great deal, for that matter, to be said for nuns. But there is nothing to be surprised at, nothing to call for any charge of inconsistency or lack of enlightenment, about the conduct of Watts and the great men of his age, in being unable to separate art from ethics. They were nationalists and universalists: they thought that the ecstatic isolation of the religious sense had done incalculable harm to religion. It is not remarkable or unreasonable that they should think that the ecstatic isolation of the artistic sense would do incalculable harm to art.

This, then, was the atmosphere of Watts and

Victorian idealism: an atmosphere so completely vanished from the world of art in which we now live, that the above somewhat long introduction is really needed to make it vivid or human to us. These three elements may legitimately, as I have said, be predicated of it as its main characteristics: first, the sceptical idealism, the belief that abstract verities remained the chief affairs of men when theology left them; second, the didactic simplicity, the claim to teach other men and to assume one's own value and rectitude; third, the cosmic utilitarianism, the consideration of any such thing as art or philosophy perpetually with reference to a general good. They may be right or wrong, they may be returning or gone for ever; theories and fashions may change the face of humanity again and yet again; but at least in that one old man at Limnerslease, burn, and will burn until death, these convictions, like three lamps in an old pagan temple of stoicism.

Of the ancestry of Watts so little is known that it resolves itself into one hypothesis: a hypothesis which brings with it a suggestion, a suggestion employed by almost all his existing

biographers, but a suggestion which cannot, I
think, pass unchallenged although the matter
may appear somewhat theoretic and remote.
Watts was born in London, but his family had
in the previous generation come from Hereford.
The vast amount of Welsh blood which is by
the nature of the case to be found in Hereford-
shire, has led to the statement that Watts is
racially a Celt, which is very probably true.
But it is also said, in almost every notice of his
life and work, that the Celtic spirit can be detected in his painting, that the Celtic principle
of mysticism is a characteristic of his artistic
conceptions. It is in no idly antagonistic spirit
that I venture to doubt this most profoundly.
Watts may or may not be racially a Celt, but
there is nothing Celtic about his mysticism.
The essential Celtic spirit in letters and art
may, I think, be defined as a sense of the un-
bearable beauty of things. The essential spirit
of Watts may, I think, be much better expressed
as a sense of the joyful austerity of things. The
dominant passion of the artistic Celt of Mr W.
B. Yeats or Sir Edward Burne-Jones, is in the
word " escape " : escape into a land where
oranges grow on plum trees and men can sow

THE SLUMBER OF THE AGES

what they like and reap what they enjoy. To Watts the very word "escape" would be horrible, like an obscene word : his ideal is altogether duty and the great wheel. To the Celt, frivolity is most truly the most serious of things, since in the tangle of roses is always the old serpent who is wiser than the world. To Watts, seriousness is most truly the most "joyful of things," since in it we come nearest to that ultimate equilibrium and reconciliation of things whereby alone they live and endure life and each other. It is difficult to imagine that amid all the varieties of noble temper and elemental desire there could possibly be two exhibiting a more total divergence than that between a kindly severity and an almost cruel love of sweetness ; than that between a laborious and open-air charity and a kind of Bacchic asceticism ; between a joy in peace and a joy in disorder ; between a reduction of existence to its simplest formula and an extension of it to its most frantic corollary ; between a lover of justice who accepts the real world more submissively than a slave and a lover of pleasure who despises the real world more bitterly than a hermit ; between a king in battle-harness and a vagabond in elf-land; between Watts and Sir Edward Burne-Jones.

It is remarkable that even the technical style of Watts gives a contradiction to this Celtic theory. Watts is strong precisely where the Celt is weak, and weak precisely where the Celt is strong. The only thing that the Celt has lacked in art is that hard mass, that naked outline, that ἀρχιτεκτονική, which makes Watts a sort of sculptor of draughtsmanship. It is as well for us that the Celt has not had this: if he had, he would rule the world with a rod of iron: for he has everything else. There are no hard black lines in Burke's orations, or Tom Moore's songs, or the plays of Mr W. B. Yeats. Burke is the greatest of political philosophers, because in him only are there distances and perspectives, as there are on the real earth, with its mists of morning and evening, and its blue horizons and broken skies. Moore's songs have neither a pure style nor deep realisation, nor originality of form, nor thought nor wit nor vigour, but they have something else which is none of these things, which is nameless and the one thing needful. In Mr Yeats' plays there is only one character: the hero who rules and kills all the others, and his name is Atmosphere. Atmosphere and the gleaming distances are the soul of Celtic greatness as they were of Burne-Jones, who was, as I have said, weak precisely where Watts is strong, in the statuesque quality in drawing, in the love of heavy hands like those of *Mammon*, of a strong back like that of *Eve Repentant*, in a single fearless and austere outline like that of the angel in *The Court of Death*, in the frame-filling violence of *Jonah*, in the half-witted brutality of *The Minotaur*. He is deficient, that is to say, in what can only be called the god-like materialism of art. Watts, on the other hand, is peculiarly strong in it. Idealist as he is, there is nothing frail or phantasmal about the things or the figures he loves. Though not himself a robust man, he loves robustness; he loves a great bulk of shoulder, an abrupt bend of neck, a gigantic stride, a large and swinging limb, a breast bound as with bands of brass. Of course the deficiency in such a case is very far from being altogether on one side. There are abysses in Burne-Jones which Watts could not understand, the Celtic madness, older than any sanity, the hunger that will remain after the longest feast, the sorrow that is built up of stratified delights. From the point of view of the true Celt, Watts, the Watts who painted the great stoical pictures *Love and Death, Time Death and Judgment, The Court of Death, Mammon* and *Cain,* this pictorial Watts would probably be, must almost certainly be, simply a sad, sane, strong, stupid Englishman. He may or may not be Welsh by extraction or by part of his extraction, but in spirit he is an Englishman, with all the faults and all the disadvantages of an Englishman. He is a great Englishman like Milton or Gladstone, of the type, that is to say, that were too much alive for anything but gravity, and who enjoyed themselves far too much to trouble to enjoy a joke. Matthew Arnold has come near to defining that kind of idealism, so utterly different from the Celtic kind, which is to be found in Milton and again in Watts. He has called it, in one of his finest and most accurate phrases, "the imaginative reason."

This racial legend about the Watts family does not seem to rest upon any certain foundations, and as I have said, the deduction drawn from it is quite loose and misleading.

CARDINAL MANNING

The whole is only another example of that unfortunate, if not infamous, modern habit of talking about such things as heredity with a vague notion that science has closed the question when she has only just opened it. Nobody knows, as a matter of fact, whether a Celtic mysticism can be inherited any more than a theory on the Education Bill. But the eagerness of the popular mind to snatch at a certainty is too impatient for the tardy processes of real hypothesis and research. Long before heredity has become a science, it has become a superstition. And this curious, though incidental case of the origin of the Watts genius, is just one of those cases which make us wonder what has been the real result of the great rise of science. So far the result would painfully appear to be that whereas men in the earlier times said unscientific things with the vagueness of gossip and legend, they now say unscientific things with the plainness and the certainty of science.

The actual artistic education of Watts, though thorough indeed in its way, had a somewhat peculiar character, the air of something detached and private, and to the external eye, something even at random. He works hard, but in an elusive and personal manner. He does not remember the time when he did not draw : he was an artist in his babyhood as he is an artist still in his old age. Like Ruskin and many other of the great and serious men of the century, he would seem to have been brought up chiefly on what may be called the large legendary literature, on such men as Homer and Scott. Among his earliest recorded works was a set of coloured illustrations to the Waverley Novels, and a sketch of the struggle for the body of Patroclus. He went to the Academy schools, but only stayed there about a month ; never caring for or absorbing the teaching, such as it was, of the place. He wandered perpetually in the Greek galleries of the British Museum, staring at the Elgin marbles, from which he has always declared he learnt all the art he knows. " There," he said, stretching out his hand towards the Ilyssus in his studio, " There is my master." We hear of a friendship between him and the sculptor William Behnes, of Watts lounging about that artist's studio, playing with clay, modelling busts, and staring at the work of sculpture. His eyes seemed to have been at this time the largest and hungriest part of him. Even when the great chance and first triumph of his life arrived a year or two later, even when he gained the great scholarship which sent him abroad to work amid the marbles of Italy, when a famous ambassador was his patron and a brilliant circle his encouragement, we do not find anything of the conventional student about him. He never painted in the galleries; he only dreamed in them. This must not, of course, be held to mean that he did not work; though one or two people who have written memoirs of Watts have used a phraseology, probably without noticing it, which might be held to imply this. Not only is the thing ludicrously incongruous with his exact character and morals; but anyone who knows anything whatever about the nature of pictorial art, will know quite well that a man could not paint like that without having worked; just as he would know that a man could not be the Living Serpent without any previous practice with his joints. To say that he could really learn to paint and draw with the technical merit of

Watts, or with any technical merit at all, by simply looking at other people's pictures and statues will seem to anyone, with a small technical sense, like saying that a man learnt to be a sublime violinist by staring at fiddles in a shop window. It is as near a physical impossibility as can exist in these matters. Work Watts must have done and did do; it is the only conclusion possible, which is consistent either with the nature of Watts or the nature of painting; and it is fully supported by the facts. But what the facts do reveal is that he worked in this curiously individual, this curiously invisible way. He had his own notion of when to dream and when to draw; as he shrank from no toil, so he shrank from no idleness. He was something which is one of the most powerful and successful things in the world, something which is far more powerful and successful than a legion of students and prizemen: he was a serious and industrious truant.

It is worth while to note this in his boyhood, partly, of course, because from one end of his life to the other there is this queer note of loneliness and liberty. But it is also more

CHAOS

immediately and practically important because it throws some light on the development and character of his art, and even especially of his technique. The great singularity of Watts, considered as a mere artist, is that he stands alone. He is not connected with any of the groups of the nineteenth century: he has neither followed a school nor founded one. He is not mediæval; but no one could exactly call him classical: we have only to compare him to Leighton to feel the difference at once. His artistic style is rather a thing more primitive than paganism; a thing to which paganism and mediævalism are alike upstart sects; a style of painting there might have been upon the tower of Babel. He is mystical; but he is not mediæval: we have only to compare him to Rossetti to feel the difference. When he emerged into the artistic world, that world was occupied by the pompous and historical school, that school which was so exquisitely caricatured by Thackeray in Gandish and his "Boadishia"; but Watts was not pompous or historical: he painted one historical picture, which brought him a youthful success, and he has scarcely painted another.

He lived on through the great Pre-Raphaelite time, that very noble and very much under-valued time, when men found again what had been hidden since the thirteenth century under loads of idle civilisation, the truth that sim-plicity and a monastic laboriousness is the happiest of all things; the great truth that purity is the only atmosphere for passion; the great truth that silver is more beautiful than gold. But though there is any quantity of this senti-ment in Watts himself, Watts never has been a Pre-Raphaelite. He has seen other fashions come and go; he has seen the Pre-Raphaelites overwhelmed by a heavy restoration of the conventional, headed by Millais with his Scotch moors and his English countesses; but he has not heeded it. He has seen these again over-turned by the wild lancers of Whistler; he has seen the mists of Impressionism settle down over the world, making it weird and delicate and non-committal: but he thinks no more of the wet mist of the Impressionist than he thought of the dry glare of the Pre-Raphaelite.

He, the most mild of men, has yet never been anything but Watts. He has followed the gleam, like some odd modern Merlin. He has escaped all the great atmospheres, the divine, if deluding intoxications, which have whirled one man one way and one another; which flew to the head of a perfect stylist like Ruskin and made him an insane scientist; which flew to the head of a great artist like Whistler and made him a pessimistic dandy. He has passed them with a curious immunity, an immunity which if it were not so nakedly innocent, might almost be called egotism; but which is in fact rather the single eye. He said once that he had not even consented to illustrate a book; his limitation was that he could express no ideas but his own. He admired Tennyson; he thought him the greatest of poets; he thought him a far greater man than himself; he read him, he adored him, but he could not illustrate him. This is the curious secret strength which kept him independent in his youth and kept him independent through the great roaring triumph of the Pre-Raphaelite and the great roaring triumph of the Impressionist. He stands in the world of art as he stood in the studio of Behnes and in the Uffizi Gallery. He stands gazing, but not copying.

GEORGE FREDERICK WATTS

Of Watts as ne was at this time there remains a very interesting portrait painted by himself. It represents him at the age of nineteen, a dark, slim, and very boyish looking creature. Something in changed conditions may no doubt account for the flowing and voluminous dark hair: we see such a mane in many of the portraits of the most distinguished men of that time; but if a man appeared now and walked down Fleet Street with so neglected a *hure,* he would be mistaken for an advertisement of a hair-dresser, or by the more malicious, for a minor poet. But there is about this picture not a trace of affectation or the artistic immunity in these matters: the boy's dress is rough and ordinary, his expression is simple and unconscious. From a modern standpoint we should say without hesitation that if his hair is long it is because he has forgotten to have it cut. And there is something about this contrast between the unconsciously leonine hair and the innocent and almost bashful face, there is something like a parable of Watts. His air is artistic, if you will. His famous skull cap, which makes him look like a Venetian senator, is as pictorial and

"FOR HE HAD GREAT POSSESSIONS"

effective as the boyish mane in the picture.
But he belongs to that older race of Bohemians,
of which even Thackeray only saw the sunset,
the great old race of art and literature who were
ragged because they were really poor, frank
because they were really free, and untidy
because they were really forgetful. It will not
do to confuse Watts with these men ; there is
much about him that is precise and courtly,
and which, as I shall have occasion to remark,
belongs really to a yet older period. But it is
more right to reckon Watts along with them
in their genuine raggedness, than to suppose
that the unquestionable picturesqueness with
which he fronts the world has any relation with
that new Bohemianism which is untidy because
it is conventional, frank because it follows a
fashion, careless because it watches for all its
effects, and ragged and coarse in its tastes
because it has too much money.

The first definite encouragement or at least
the first encouragement now ascertainable, probably came to the painter from that interesting
Greek amateur, Mr Constantine Ionides. It was
under his encouragement that Watts began all
his earlier work of the more ambitious kind,

and it was the portrait of Mrs Constantine Ionides which ranks among the earliest of his definite successes. He achieved immediate professional success, however, at an astonishingly early age, judged by modern standards. When he was barely twenty, he had three pictures in the Royal Academy, the first two were portraits and the third a picture called *The Wounded Heron*. There is always a very considerable temptation to fantasticality in dealing with these artistic origins: no doubt it does not always follow that a man is destined to be a military conqueror because he beats other little boys at school, nor endued with a passionate and clamorous nature because he begins this mortal life with a yell. But Watts has, to a rather unusual degree, a sincere and consistent and homogeneous nature; and this first exhibit of his has really a certain amount of symbolism about it. Portraiture, with which he thus began, he was destined to raise to a level never before attained in English art, so far as significance and humanity are concerned; and there is really something a little fascinating about the fact that along with these pictures went one picture which had, for all practical purposes, an avowedly humanitarian object. The picture of *The Wounded Heron* scarcely ever attracts attention, I imagine, in these days, but it may, of course, have been recalled for a moment to the popular mind by that curious incident which occurred in connection with it and which has often been told. Long after the painter who produced that picture in his struggling boyhood had lost sight of and in all probability forgotten all about its existence, a chance traveller with a taste in the arts happened to find it in the dusty curiosity-shop of a north country town. He bought it and gave it back to the now celebrated painter, who has hung it among the exhibits at Little Holland House. It is, as I have said, a thing painted clearly with a humanitarian object : it depicts the suffering of a stricken creature; it depicts the helplessness of life under the cruelty of the inanimate violence ; it depicts the pathos of dying and the greater pathos of living. Since then, no doubt, Watts has improved his machinery of presentation and found larger and more awful things to tell his tale with than a bleeding bird. The wings of the heron have widened till they embrace the world with the terrible wings of Time or Death: he has summoned the stars to help him and sent the angels as his ambassadors. He has changed the plan of operations until it includes Heaven and Tartarus. He has never changed the theme.

The relations of Watts to Constantine Ionides either arose or became important about this time. The painter's fortunes rose quickly and steadily, so far as the Academy was concerned. He continued to exhibit with a fair amount of regularity, chiefly in the form of subjects from the great romantic or historic traditions which were then the whole pabulum of the young idealistic artist. In the Academy of 1840 came a picture on the old romantic subject of Ferdinand and Isabella; in the following year but one, a picture on the old romantic subject of Cymbeline. The portrait of Mrs Constantine Ionides appeared in 1842.

But Watts' mode of thought from the very beginning had very little kinship with the Academy and very little kinship with this kind of private and conventional art. An event was shortly to occur, the first success of his life, but an event far less important when considered as

AN IDLE CHILD OF FANCY

wd

the first success of his life than it is when considered as an essential characteristic of his mind. The circumstances are so extremely characteristic of something in the whole spirit of the man's art, that it may be permissible to dwell at length on the significance of the fact rather than on the fact itself.

The great English Parliament, the Senate that broke the English kings, had just moved its centre of existence. The new Houses of Parliament had opened with what seemed to the men of that time an opening world. A competition was started for the decoration of the halls, and Watts suddenly sprang into importance : he won the great prize. The cartoon of *Caractacus led in triumph through the streets of Rome* was accepted from this almost nameless man by the great central power of English history. And until we have understood that fact we have not understood Watts : it was (one may be permitted to fancy) the supreme hour of his life. For Watts' nature is essentially public, that is to say, it is modest and noble, and has nothing to hide. His art is an out-door art, like that of the healthy ages of the world, like the statuesque art of Greece, like the ecclesiastical and external Gothic art of Christianity: an art that can look the sun in the face.   He ought to be employed to paint factory chimneys and railway-stations.   I know that this will sound like an insolence: my only answer is that he, in accordance with this great conception of his, actually offered to paint a railway-station. With a splendid and truly religious imagination, he asked permission to decorate Euston.   The railway managers (not perceiving, in their dull classical routine, the wild poetry of their own station) declined.   But until we have understood this immense notion of publicity in the soul of Watts, we have understood nothing. The fundamental modern fallacy is that the public life must be an artificial life.   It is like saying that the public street must be an artificial air.   Men like Watts, men like all the great heroes, only breathe in public. What is the use of abusing a man for publicity when he utters in public the true and the enduring things?   What is the use, above all, of prying into his secrecy, when he has cried his best from the housetops?

This is the real argument which makes a

detailed biography of Watts unnecessary for
all practical purposes. It is in vain to climb
walls and hide in cupboards in order to show
whether Watts eats mustard or pepper with his
curry or whether Watts takes sugar or salt
with his porridge. These things may or may
not become public : it matters little. The
innermost that the biographer could at last
discover, after all possible creepings and
capers, would be what Watts in his inmost
soul believes, and that Watts has splashed on
twenty feet of canvas and given to the nation
for nothing. Like one of the great orators of
the eighteenth century, his public virtues, his
public ecstasies are far more really significant
than his private weaknesses. The rest of his
life is so simple that it is scarcely worth telling.
He went with the great scholarship he gained
with his *Caractacus* to Italy. There he found
a new patron—the famous Lord Holland, with
the whole of whose great literary circle he
rapidly became acquainted. He painted many
of his most famous portraits in connection with
this circle, both in Italy and afterwards in
Paris. But this great vision of the public idea
had entered his blood. He offered his cartoons

to Euston Station ; he painted St George and
the Dragon for the House of Lords ; he
presented a fresco to the great hall at Lin-
coln's Inn. Of his life there is scarcely more
to say, except the splendid fact that he has
three times refused a title. Of his character
there is a great deal more to say.

There is unquestionably about the personal
attitude of Watts, something that in the vague
phraseology of modern times would be called
Puritan. Puritan, however, is very far from
being really the right word. The right word
is a word which has been singularly little
used in English nomenclature because historical
circumstances have separated us from the
origin from which it sprang. The right word
for the spirit of Watts is *Stoicism*. Watts
is at one with the Puritans in the actual
objects of his attack. One of his deepest and
most enduring troubles, a matter of which he
speaks and writes frequently, is the prevalence
of gambling. With the realism of an en-
thusiast, he has detected the essential fact
that the problem of gambling is even more
of a problem in the case of the poorer classes
than in the case of the richer. It is, as he

THE MINOTAUR

asserts, a far worse danger than drink. There are many other instances of his political identity with Puritanism. He told Mr W. T. Stead that he had defended and was prepared to defend the staggering publications of the " Maiden Tribute " ; it was the only way, he said, to stem the evil. A picturesque irradiation asserts indeed that it was under the glow of Hebraic anger against these Babylonian cruelties of Piccadilly and the Strand that he painted as a symbol of those cruelties, that brutal and magnificent picture *The Minotaur*. The pictures themselves of course bear sufficient attestation to this general character : *Mammon* is what we call a Puritan picture, and *Jonah*, and *Fata Morgana* and *For he had Great Possessions*. It is not difficult to see that Watts has the Puritan vigilance, the Puritan realism, and the Puritan severity in his attitude towards public affairs. Nevertheless, as I have said, he is to be described rather as a Stoic than a Puritan. The essential difference between Christian and Pagan asceticism lies in the fact that Paganism in renouncing pleasure, gives up something which it does not think desirable ; whereas Christianity in giving up pleasure gives up something which it thinks very desirable indeed. Thus there is a frenzy in Christian asceticism; its follies and renunciations are like those of first love. There is a passion, and as it were a regret in the Puritanism of Bunyan; there is none in the Puritanism of Watts. He is not Bunyan, he is Cato. The difference may be a difficult one to convey, but it is one that must not be ignored or great misunderstandings will follow. The one self-abnegation is more reasonable but less joyful. The Stoic casts away pleasure like the parings of his nails; the Mystic cuts it off like his right hand that offends him. In Watts, we have the noble self-abnegation of a noble type and school; but everything, however noble, that has shape has limitation, and we must not look in Watts, with his national self-mastery, either for the nightmare of Stylites or the gaiety of Francis of Assisi.

It has already been remarked that the chief note of the painter's character is a certain mixture of personal delicacy and self-effacement with the most immense and audacious aims. But it is so essential a trait that it will bear a repetition and the introduction of a curious example of it. Watts in his quaint and even shy manner of speech has often let fall in conversation words which hint at a certain principle or practice of his, a principle and practice which are, when properly apprehended, beyond expression impressive and daring. The spectator who studies his allegorical paintings one after another will be vaguely impressed with something uniquely absent, something which is usual and familiar in such pictures conspicuous by its withdrawal; a blank or difference which makes them things sundered altogether from the millions of allegorical pictures that throng the great and small galleries of painting. At length the nature of this missing thing may suddenly strike him: in the whole range of Watts' symbolic art there is scarcely a single example of the ordinary and arbitrary current symbol, the ecclesiastical symbol, the heraldic symbol, the national symbol. A primeval vagueness and archaism hangs over all the canvases and cartoons, like frescoes from some prehistoric temple. There is nothing there but the eternal things, clay and fire and the sea, and

motherhood and the dead. We cannot imagine
the rose or the lion of England; the keys or
the tiara of Rome; the red cap of Liberty or
the crescent of Islam in a picture by Watts; we
cannot imagine the Cross itself. And in light
and broken phrases, carelessly and humbly
expressed, as I have said, the painter has
admitted that this great omission was ob-
served on principle. Its object is that the
pictures may be intelligible if they survive the
whole modern order. Its object is, that is to
say, that if some savage in a dim futurity dug
up one of these dark designs on a lonely
mountain, though he worshipped strange gods
and served laws yet unwritten, it might strike
the same message to his soul that it strikes
upon clerks and navvies from the walls of the
Tate Gallery. It is impossible not to feel a
movement of admiration for the magnitude of
the thought. Here is a man whose self-
depreciation is internal and vital; whose life
is cloistered, whose character is child-like, and
he has yet within such unconscious and colossal
sense of greatness that he paints on the
assumption that his work may outlast the cross
of the Eternal City. As a boy he scarcely

THE COURT OF DEATH

expected worldly success : as an old man he still says that his worldly success has astonished him. But in his nameless youth and in his silent old age, he paints like one upon a tower looking down the appalling perspective of the centuries towards fantastic temples and inconceivable republics.

This union of small self-esteem with a vast ambition is a paradox in the very soul of the painter ; and when we look at the symbolic pictures in the light of this theory of his, it is interesting and typical to observe how consistently he pursues any intellectual rule that he has laid down for himself. An æsthetic or ethical notion of this kind is not to him, as to most men with the artistic temperament, a thing to talk about sumptuously, to develop in lectures and to observe when it happens to be suitable. It is a thing like his early rising or his personal conscience, a thing which is either a rule or nothing. And we find this insistence on universal symbols, this rejection of all symbols that are local or temporary or topical, even if the locality be a whole continent, the time a stretch of centuries, or the topic a vast civilisation or an undying church, we find this insistence looking out very clearly from the allegories of Watts. It would have been easy and effective, as he himself has often said, to make the meaning of a picture clear by the introduction of some popular and immediate image : and it must constantly be remembered that Watts does care very much for making the meaning of his pictures clear. His work indeed has, as I shall suggest shortly, a far more subtle and unnameable quality than the merely hard and didactic ; but it must not be for one moment pretended that Watts does not claim to teach : to do so would be to falsify the man's life. And it would be easy, as is quite obvious, to make the pictures clearer : to hang a crucifix over the *Happy Warrior,* to give *Mammon* some imperial crown or typical heraldic symbols, to give a theological machinery to *The Court of Death.* But this is put on one side like a temptation of the flesh, because it conflicts with this stupendous idea of painting for all peoples and all centuries. I am not saying that this extraordinary ambition is necessarily the right view of art, or the right view of life. I am only reiterating it as an absolute trait of men of the time and type and temper of Watts. It may plausibly be maintained, I am not sure that it cannot more truly be maintained, that man cannot achieve and need not achieve this frantic universality. A man, I fancy, is after all only an animal that has noble preferences. It is the very difference between the artistic mind and the mathematical that the former sees things as they are in a picture, some nearer and larger, some smaller and further away: while to the mathematical mind everything, every unit in a million, every fact in a cosmos, must be of equal value. That is why mathematicians go mad; and poets scarcely ever do. A man may have as wide a view of life as he likes, the wider the better; a distant view, a bird's eye view, if he will, but still a view and not a map. The one thing he cannot attempt in his version of the universe is to draw things to scale. I have put myself for a moment outside this universalism and doubted its validity, because a thing always appears more sharp and personal and picturesque if we do not wholly agree with it. And this universalism is an essential and dominant feature of such great men as Watts and of his time as a whole. Mr Herbert Spencer is a respectable, almost a dapper figure, his theory is agnostic and his tone polite and precise. And yet he threw himself into a task more insane and gigantic than that of Dante, an inventory or plan of the universe itself; the awful vision of existence as a single organism, like an amœba on the disc of a microscope. He claimed, by implication, to put in their right places the flaming certainty of the martyrs, the wild novelties of the modern world; to arrange the eternal rock of Peter and the unbroken trance of Buddhism. It is only in this age of specialists, of cryptic experiences in art and faith, like the present, that we can see how huge was that enterprise; but the spirit of it is the spirit of Watts. The man of that aggressive nineteenth century had many wild thoughts, but there was one thought that never even for an instant strayed across his burning brain. He never once thought, "Why should I understand the cat, any more than the cat understands me?" He never thought, "Why should I be just to the merits of a Chinaman, any more than a pig studies the mystic virtues of a camel?" He affronted heaven and the angels, but there was one hard arrogant dogma that he never

MATTHEW ARNOLD

doubted even when he doubted Godhead : he never doubted that he himself was as central and as responsible as God.

This paradox, then, we call the first element in the artistic and personal claim of Watts, that he realises the great paradox of the Gospel. He is meek, but he claims to inherit the earth. But there is, of course, a great deal more to be said before this view of the matter can be considered complete. The universalism preached by Watts and the other great Victorians was of course subject to certain specialisations ; it is not necessary to call them limitations. Like Matthew Arnold, the last and most sceptical of them, who expressed their basic idea in its most detached and philosophic form, they held that conduct was three-fourths of life. They were ingrainedly ethical ; the mere idea of thinking anything more important than ethics would have struck them as profane. In this they were certainly right, but they were nevertheless partial or partisan ; they did not really maintain the judicial attitude of the universalist. The mere thought of Watts painting a picture called *The Victory of Joy over Morality*, or *Nature rebuking Conscience,* is enough to show the definite limits of that cosmic equality. This is not, of course, to be taken as a fault in the attitude of Watts. He simply draws the line somewhere, as all men, including anarchists, draw it somewhere ; he is dogmatic as all sane men are dogmatic.

There is another phase of this innocent audacity. It may appear to be more fanciful, it is certainly more completely a matter of inference ; but it throws light on yet another side of the character of Watts.

Watts' relation to friends and friendship has something about it very typical. He is not a man desirous or capable of a very large or rich or varied circle of acquaintance. There is nothing Bohemian about him. He belongs both chronologically and psychologically to that period which is earlier even than Thackeray and his Cave of Harmony : he belongs to the quiet, struggling, self-created men of the '40's, with their tradition of self-abnegating individualism. Much as there is about him of the artist and the poet, there is something about him also of the industrious apprentice. That strenuous solitude in which Archbishop Temple as a boy struggled to carry a bag of ironmongery

JOHN STUART MILL

which crushed his back, in which Gladstone cut down trees and John Stuart Mill read half the books of the world in boyhood, that strenuous solitude has entered to some degree into the very soul of Watts and made him independent of men. But the friends he has made, have as a general rule been very characteristic: they have marked the strange and haughty fastidiousness that goes along with his simplicity. His friends, his intimate friends, that is, have been marked by a certain indescribable and stately worthiness: more than one of them have been great men like himself. The greatest and most intimate of all his friends, probably, was Tennyson, and in this there is something singularly characteristic of Watts. About the actuality of the intellectual tie that bound him to Tennyson there can be little doubt. He has painted three if not four portraits of him; his name is often on his lips; he invokes him always as the typical great poet, excusing his faults and expounding his virtues. He invoked his authority as that of the purest of poets, and invoked it very finely and well in a sharp controversial interview he had on the nature and ethics of the nude in art. At the time I write, there is standing at the end of the garden at Limnerslease, a vast shed, used for a kind of sculptor's studio, in which there stands a splendid but unfinished statue, on which the veteran of the arts is even now at work. It represents Tennyson, wrapped in his famous mantle, with his magnificent head bowed, gazing at something in the hollow of his hand. The subject is *Flower in the Crannied Wall.* There is something very characteristic of Watts in the contrast between the colossal plan of the figure and the smallness of the central object.

But while the practical nature of the friendship between Watts and Tennyson is clear enough, there is something really significant, something really relevant to Watts' attitude, in its ultimate and psychological character. It is surely most likely that Watts and Tennyson were drawn together because they both represented a certain relation towards their art which is not common in our time and was scarcely properly an attribute of any artists except these two. Watts could not have found the thing he most believed in Browning or Swinburne or Morris or any of the

ROBERT BROWNING

other poets. Tennyson could not have found the thing he most believed in Leighton or Millais or any of the other painters. They were brought together, it must be supposed, by the one thing that they had really in common, a profound belief in the solemnity, the ceremoniousness, the responsibility and what most men would now, in all probability, call the pomposity of the great arts.

Watts has always a singular kind of semi-mystical tact in the matter of portrait painting. His portraits are commonly very faultless comments and have the same kind of superlative mental delicacy that we see in the picture of *Hope*. And the whole truth of this last matter is very well expressed in Watts' famous portrait of Tennyson, particularly if we look at it in conjunction with his portrait of Browning. The head of Browning is the head of a strong, splendid, joyful and anxious man who could write magnificent poetry. The head of Tennyson is the head of a poet. Watts has painted Tennyson, with his dark dome-like head relieved against a symbolic green and blue of the eternal sea and the eternal laurels. He has behind him the bays of Dante and he is wrapped

in the cloak of the prophets. Browning is
dressed like an ordinary modern man, and we
at once feel that it should and must be so. To
dress Browning in the prophet's robe and the
poet's wreath would strike us all as suddenly
ridiculous ; it would be like sending him to a
fancy dress ball. It would be like attiring
Matthew Arnold in the slashed tights of an
Elizabethan, or putting Mr Lecky into a
primitive Celto-Irish kilt. But it does not
strike us as absurd in the case of Tennyson : it
does not strike us as even eccentric or outlandish or remote. We think of Tennyson
in that way ; we think of him as a lordly and
conscious bard. Some part of this fact may,
of course, be due to his possession of a magnificent physical presence ; but not, I think, all.
Lord Kitchener (let us say) is a handsome man,
but we should laugh at him very much in silver
armour. It is much more due to the fact that
Tennyson really assumed and was granted this
stately and epic position. It is not true that
Tennyson was more of a poet than Browning,
if we mean by that statement that Browning
could not compose forms as artistic and well-
managed, lyrics as light and poignant, and

LORD TENNYSON

rhythms as swelling and stirring as any in English letters. But it is true that Tennyson was more of a poet than Browning, if we mean by that statement that Tennyson was a poet in person, in post and circumstance and conception of life ; and that Browning was not, in that sense, a poet at all. Browning first inaugurated in modern art and letters the notion or tradition, in many ways perhaps a more wholesome one, that the fact that a man pursued the trade or practice of poetry was his own affair and a thing apart, like the fact that he collected coins or earned his living as a hatter. But Tennyson really belonged to an older tradition, the tradition that believed that the poet, the appointed " Vates," was a recognised and public figure like the bard or jester at the mediæval courts, like the prophet in the old Commonwealth of Israel. In Tennyson's work appeared for the last time in English history this notion of the stately and public and acknowledged poet : it was the lay of the last minstrel.

Now there is in Watts, gentle and invisible as he is, something that profoundly responds to that spirit. Leighton, like Browning, was a

courtier and man of the world: Millais, like
Browning, was a good fellow and an ordinary
gentleman: but Watts has more of Tennyson
in him; he believes in a great priesthood of
art. He believes in a certain pure and childish
publicity. If anyone suggested that before a
man ventured to paint pictures or to daub with
plaster he should be initiated with some awful
rites in some vast and crowded national temple,
should swear to work worthily before some
tremendous altar or over some symbolic flame,
Millais would have laughed heartily at the idea
and Leighton also. But it would not seem
either absurd or unreasonable to Watts. In
the thick of this smoky century he is living in
a clear age of heroes.

Watts' relations to Tennyson were indeed
very characteristic of what was finest, and at
the same time quaintest, in the two men. The
painter, with a typical sincerity, took the poet
seriously, I had almost said literally, in his
daily life, and liked him to live up to his
poetry. The poet with that queer sulky
humour, which gave him, perhaps, more breadth
than Watts, but less strength, said, after reading some acid and unjust criticisms, " I wish

I had never written a line." "Come," said
Watts, "you wouldn't like 'King Arthur' to
talk like that." Tennyson paused a moment
and then spread out his fingers. "Well," he
said, "what do you expect? It's all the gout."
The artist, with a characteristic power of
juvenile and immortal hero-worship, tells this
story as an instance of the fundamental
essence of odd magnanimity and sombre geni-
ality in Tennyson. It is such an instance
and a very good one : but it is also an instance
of the sharp logical idealism, of the prompt
poetic candour of Watts. He asked Tennyson
to be King Arthur, and it never occurred to
him to think that he was asking Addison to be
Cato, or Massinger to be Saint Dorothy. The
incident is a fine tribute to a friendship.

The real difficulty which many cultivated
people have, in the matter of Watts' allegorical
pictures, is far more difficult. It is indeed
nothing else but the great general reaction
against allegorical art which has arisen during
the last artistic period. The only way in
which we can study, with any real sincerity,
the allegoric art of Watts, is to ask to what is
really due the objection to allegory which has

thus arisen. The real objection to allegory is, it may roughly be said, founded upon the conception that allegory involves one art imitating another. This is, up to a certain point, true. To paint a figure in a blue robe and call her Necessity, and then paint a small figure in a yellow robe and call it Invention ; to put the second on the knee of the first, and then say that you are enunciating the sublime and eternal truth, that Necessity is the mother of Invention, this is indeed an idle and foolish affair. It is saying in six weeks' work with brush and palette-knife what could be said much better in six words. And there can be no reasonable dispute that of this character were a considerable number of the allegorical pictures that have crowded the galleries and sprawled over the ceilings of ancient and modern times. Of such were the monstrous pictures of Rubens, which depicted a fat Religion and a bloated Temperance dancing before some foreign conqueror ; of such were the florid designs of the eighteenth century, which showed Venus and Apollo encouraging Lord Peterborough to get over the inconvenience of his breastplate ; of such, again, were the

THE DWELLER IN THE INNERMOST

meek Victorian allegories which showed Mercy
and Foresight urging men to found a Society
for the Preservation of Young Game. Of such
were almost all the allegories which have
dominated the art of Europe for many
centuries back. Of such, most emphatically,
the allegories of Watts are not. They are
not mere pictorial forms, combined as in a
kind of cryptogram to express theoretic views
or relations. They are not proverbs or verbal
relations rendered with a cumbrous exactitude in
oil and Chinese white. They are not, in short,
the very thing that the opponents of Watts
and his school say that they are. They are
not merely literary. There is one definite
current conception on which this idea that
Watts' allegorical art is merely literary is
eventually based. It is based upon the idea
that lies at the root of rationalism, at the root
of useless logomachies, at the root, in no small
degree, of the whole modern evil. It is based
on the assumption of the perfection of language.
Every religion and every philosophy must, of
course, be based on the assumption of the
authority or the accuracy of something. But
it may well be questioned whether it is not

saner and more satisfactory to ground our faith on the infallibility of the Pope, or the infallibility of the Book of Mormon, than on this astounding modern dogma of the infallibility of human speech. Every time one man says to another. "Tell us plainly what you mean?" he is assuming the infallibility of language : that is to say, he is assuming that there is a perfect scheme of verbal expression for all the internal moods and meanings of men. Whenever a man says to another, "Prove your case ; defend your faith," he is assuming the infallibility of language : that is to say, he is assuming that a man has a word for every reality in earth, or heaven, or hell. He knows that there are in the soul tints more bewildering, more numberless and more nameless, than the colours of an autumn forest ; he knows that there are abroad in the world and doing strange and terrible service in it, crimes that have never been condemned and virtues that have never been christened. Yet he seriously believes that these things can every one of them, in all their tones and semi-tones, in all their blends and unions, be accurately represented by an arbitrary system of grunts

GEORGE MEREDITH

and squeals. He believes that an ordinary
civilised stockbroker can really produce out
of his own inside, noises which denote all the
mysteries of memory and all the agonies of
desire. Whenever, on the other hand, a man
rebels faintly or vaguely against this way of
speaking, whenever a man says that he cannot
explain what he means, and that he hates
argument, that his enemy is misrepresenting
him, but he cannot explain how ; that man is a
true sage, and has seen into the heart of the
real nature of language. Whenever a man
refuses to be caught by some dilemma about
reason and passion, or about reason and faith,
or about fate and free-will, he has seen the
truth. Whenever a man declines to be
cornered as an egoist, or an altruist, or any
such modern monster, he has seen the truth.
For the truth is, that language is not a scientific
thing at all, but wholly an artistic thing, a
thing invented by hunters, and killers, and
such artists, long before science was dreamed
of. The truth is simply that—that the tongue
is not a reliable instrument, like a theodolite
or a camera. The tongue is most truly an
unruly member, as the wise saint has called

it, a thing poetic and dangerous, like music or fire.

Now we can easily imagine an alternative state of things, roughly similar to that produced in Watts' allegories, a system, that is to say, whereby the moods or facts of the human spirit were conveyed by something other than speech, by shapes or colours or some such things. As a matter of fact, of course, there are a great many other languages besides the verbal. Descriptions of spiritual states and mental purposes are conveyed by a variety of things, by hats, by bells, by guns, by fires on a headland or by jerks of the head. In fact there does exist an example which is singularly analogous to decorative and symbolic painting. There is a scheme of æsthetic signs or emblems, simple indeed and consisting only of a few elemental colours, which is actually employed to convey great lessons in human safety and great necessities of the Commonwealth. It need hardly be said that I allude to the railway signals. They are as much a language, and surely as solemn a language, as the colour-sequence of ecclesiastical vestments, which sets us red for martyrdom,

and white for resurrection. For the green
and red of the night-signals depict the two
most fundamental things of all, which lie at
the back of all language. Yes and no, good
and bad, safe and unsafe, life and death. It
is perfectly conceivable that a degree of flexi-
bility or subtlety might be introduced into
these colours, so as to suggest other and more
complex meanings. We might (under the
influence of some large poetic station-masters),
reach a state of things in which a certain rich
tinge of purple in the crimson light would
mean " Travel for a few seconds at a slightly
more lingering pace, that a romantic old lady
in a first-class carriage may admire the scenery
of the forest." A tendency towards peacock
blue in the green might mean " An old gentleman with a black necktie has just drunk a
glass of sherry at the station restaurant."
But however much we modified or varied this
colour sequence or colour language, there
would remain one thing which it would be
quite ridiculous and untrue to say about it.
It would be quite ridiculous and untrue to say
that this colour sequence was simply a symbol
representing language. It would be another

language: it would convey its meaning to aliens who had another word for forest and another word for sherry, and another word for old lady. It would not be a symbol of language, a symbol of a symbol, it would be one symbol of the reality, and language would be another. That is precisely the true position touching allegorical art in general, and above all, the allegorical art of Watts.

So long as we conceive that it is, fundamentally, the symbolising of literature in paint, we shall certainly misunderstand it and the rare and peculiar merits, both technical and philosophical, which really characterise it. If the ordinary spectator at the art galleries finds himself, let us say, opposite a picture of a dancing flower-crowned figure in a rose-coloured robe, he feels a definite curiosity to know the title, looks it up in the catalogue and finds that is called, let us say, " Hope." He is immediately satisfied, as he would have been if the title had run " Portrait of Lady War-wick," a "View of Kilchurn Castle." It represents a certain definite thing, the word "hope." But what does the word "hope" represent? It represents only a broken in-

ORPHEUS AND EURYDICE

stantaneous glimpse of something that is
immeasurably older and wilder than language,
that is immeasurably older and wilder than
man ; a mystery to saints and a reality to wolves.
To suppose that such a thing is dealt with
by the word "hope," any more than America
is represented by a distant view of Cape Horn,
would indeed be ridiculous.   It is not merely
true that the word itself is, like any other
word, arbitrary ; that it might as well be "pig"
or "parasol"; but it is true that the philosophical meaning of the word, in the conscious
mind of man, is merely a part of something
immensely larger in the unconscious mind,
that the gusty light of language only falls for
a moment on a fragment, and that obviously
a semi-detached, unfinished fragment of a
certain definite pattern on the dark tapestries
of reality.   It is vain and worse than vain to
declaim against the allegoric for the very
word "hope" is an allegory, and the very
word "allegory" is an allegory.

Now let us suppose that instead of coming
before that hypothetical picture of *Hope* in
conventional flowers and conventional pink
robes, the spectator came before another

picture. Suppose that he found himself in the presence of a dim canvas with a bowed and stricken and secretive figure cowering over a broken lyre in the twilight. What would he think? His first thought, of course, would be that the picture was called *Despair*; his second (when he discovered his error in the catalogue), that it has been entered under the wrong number; his third, that the painter was mad. But if we imagine that he overcame these preliminary feelings and that as he stared at that queer twilight picture, a dim and powerful sense of meaning began to grow upon him— what would he see? He would see something for which there is neither speech nor language, which has been too vast for any eye to see and too secret for any religion to utter, even as an esoteric doctrine. Standing before that picture he finds himself in the presence of a great truth. He perceives that there is something in man which is always apparently on the eve of disappearing, but never disappears, an assurance which is always apparently saying farewell and yet illimitably lingers, a string which is always stretched to snapping and yet never snaps. He perceives that the queerest

HOPE

and most delicate thing in us, the most fragile, the most fantastic, is in truth the backbone and indestructible. He knows a great moral fact: that there never was an age of assurance, that there never was an age of faith. Faith is always at a disadvantage; it is a perpetually defeated thing which survives all its conquerors. The desperate modern talk about dark days and reeling altars, and the end of Gods and angels, is the oldest talk in the world: lamentations over the growth of agnosticism can be found in the monkish sermons of the dark ages; horror at youthful impiety can be found in the Iliad. This is the thing that never deserts men and yet always, with daring diplomacy, threatens to desert them. It has indeed dwelt among and controlled all the kings and crowds, but only with the air of a pilgrim passing by. It has indeed warmed and lit men from the beginning of Eden with an unending glow, but it was the glow of an eternal sunset.

Here, in this dim picture, its trick is almost betrayed. No one can name this picture properly, but Watts who painted it, has named it *Hope*. But the point is that this title is not (as those think who call it "literary") the reality behind the symbol, but another symbol for the same thing, or to speak yet more strictly, another symbol describing another part or aspect of the same complex reality. Two men felt a swift, violent, invisible thing in the world: one said the word "hope," the other painted a picture in blue and green paint. The picture is inadequate; the word "hope" is inadequate; but between them, like two angles in the calculation of a distance, they almost locate a mystery, a mystery that for hundreds of ages has been hunted by men and evaded them. And the title is therefore not so much the substance of one of Watts' pictures, it is rather an epigram upon it. It is merely an approximate attempt to convey, by snatching up the tool of another craftsman, the direction attempted in the painter's own craft. He calls it *Hope* and that is perhaps the best title. It reminds us among other things of a fact which is too little remembered, that faith, hope and charity, the three mystical virtues of Christianity, are also the gayest of the virtues. Paganism, as I have suggested, is not gay, but rather nobly sad; the spirit of Watts, which is as a rule nobly sad also, here comes nearer perhaps than anywhere else to mysticism in the strict sense, the mysticism which is full of secret passion and belief, like that of Fra Angelico or Blake. But though Watts calls his tremendous reality *Hope*, we may call it many other things. Call it faith, call it vitality, call it the will to live, call it the religion of to-morrow morning, call it the immortality of man, call it self-love and vanity; it is the thing that explains why man survives all things and why there is no such thing as a pessimist. It cannot be found in any dictionary or rewarded in any commonwealth: there is only one way in which it can even be noticed and recognised. If there be anywhere a man who has really lost it, his face out of a whole crowd of men will strike us like a blow. He may hang himself or become Prime Minister; it matters nothing. The man is dead.

Now, of course the ordinary objection to allegory, and it is a very sound objection, can be sufficiently well stated by saying that the pictorial figures are mere arbitrary symbols of the words. An allegorist of the pompous school might paint some group of Peace and

Commerce doing something to Britannia.
There might be a figure of Commerce in a
Greek robe with a cornucopia or bag of
gold or an argosy or any other conventional
symbol. But it is surely quite evident that
such a figure is a mere sign like the word
commerce: the word might just as well be
"dandelion," and the Greek lady with the
cornucopia might just as well be a Hebrew
prophet standing on his head. It is scarcely
even a language: it is a cipher-code. Nobody
can maintain that the figure taken as a figure,
makes one think of commerce, of the forces
that effect commerce, of a thousand ports, of a
thousand streets, of a thousand warehouses
and bills of lading, of a thousand excited men
in black coats who certainly would not know
what to do with a cornucopia. If we find
ourselves gazing at some monument of the
fragile and eternal faith of man, at some
ruined chapel, at some nameless altar, at some
scrap of old Jacobin eloquence, we might
actually find our own minds moving in certain
curves that centre in the curved back of Watts'
Hope: we might almost think for ourselves of
a bowed figure in the twilight, holding to her

JONAH

breast something damaged but undestroyed. But can anyone say that by merely looking at the Stock Exchange on a busy day we should think of a Greek lady with an argosy? Can anyone say that Threadneedle Street, in itself, would inspire our minds to move in the curves which centre in a cornucopia? Can anyone say that a very stolid figure in a very outlandish drapery is anything but a purely arbitrary sign, like x or y, for such a thing as modern commerce, for the savagery of the rich, for the hunger of the satisfied, for the vast tachycardia or galloping of the heart that has fallen on all the great new centres of civilisation, for the sudden madness of all the mills of the world?

Watts' *Hope* does tell us something more about the nature of hope than we can be told by merely noticing that hope is shown in individual cases: that a man rehearses successful love speeches when he is in love, and takes a return ticket when he goes out to fight a duel. But the figure of Commerce with the cornucopia gives us less insight into what is behind commerce than we might get from reading a circular or staring out into the street. In the case of Commerce, the figure is merely a symbol of commerce, which is a symbol. In the case of Hope, the matter is quite the other way; the figure brings us nearer to something which is not a symbol, but the reality behind symbols. In the one case we go further down towards the river's delta, in the other, further up towards its fountain; that at least may be called a difference. And now, suppose that our imaginary sight-seer, who had seen so much of the pompous allegory of Commerce in her Grecian draperies, were to see, for the second time, a second picture. Suppose he saw before him a throned figure clad in splendid, heavy scarlet and gold, above the lustre and dignity of which, rose in abrupt contrast, a face like the face of a blind beast. Suppose that as this imperial thing, with closed eyes, and fat, sightless face, sat upon his magnificent seat, he let his heavy hands and feet fall, as if by a mere pulverising accident, on the naked and god-like figures of the young, on men and women. Suppose that in the background there rose straight into the air a raw and turgid smoke, as if from some invisible and horrible sacrifice, and that by one final, fantastic and triumphal touch this all destroying god and king were adorned with the ears of an ass, declaring that he was royal, imperial, irresistible, and when all is said, imbecile. Suppose that a man sick of argosies and cornucopias came before that picture, would he not say, perhaps even before he looked in the catalogue and found that the painter had called it *Mammon*, would he not say, " This is something which in spirit and in essence I have seen before, something which in spirit and in essence I have seen everywhere. That bloated, unconscious face, so heavy, so violent, so wicked, so innocent, have I not seen it at street corners, in billiard rooms, in saloon bars, laying down the law about Chartered shares or gaping at jokes about women? Those huge and smashing limbs, so weighty, so silly, so powerless and yet so powerful, have I not seen them in the pompous movements, the morbid health of the prosperous in the great cities? The hard straight pillars of that throne, have I not seen them in the hard, straight, hideous tiers of modern warehouses and factories? That tawny and sulky smoke, have I not seen it going up to heaven from all the cities of the coming world? This is no trifling with argoses and

Greek drapery. This is commerce. This is the home of the god himself. This is why men hate him, and why men fear him, and why men endure him."

Now, of course, it is at once obvious that this view would be very unjust to commerce; but that modification, as a matter of fact, very strongly supports the general theory at the moment under consideration. Commerce is really an arbitrary phrase, a thing including a million motives, from the motive which makes a man drink, to the motive which makes him reform; from the motive that makes a starving man eat a horse, to the motive which makes an idle man chase a butterfly. But whatever other spirits there are in commerce, there is, beyond all reasonable question in it, this powerful and enduring spirit which Watts has painted. There is, as a ruling element in modern life, in all life, this blind and asinine appetite for mere power. There is a spirit abroad among the nations of the earth which drives men incessantly on to destroy what they cannot understand, and to capture what they cannot enjoy. This, and not commerce, is what Watts has painted. He has painted not

MAMMON

the allegory of a great institution, but the vision of a great appetite, the vision of a great motive. It is not true that this is a picture of Commerce; but that Commerce and Watts' picture spring from the same source. There does exist a certain dark and driving force in the world; one of its products is this picture, another is Commerce. The picture is not Commerce, it is Mammon. And, indeed, so powerfully and perfectly has Watts, in this case, realised the awful being whom he was endeavouring to call up by his artistic incantation, that we may even say the common positions of allegory and reality are reversed. The fact is not that here we have an effective presentation under a certain symbol of red robes and smoke and a throne, of what the financial world is, but rather that here we have something of the truth that is hidden behind the symbol of white waistcoats and hats on the back of the head, of financial papers and sporting prophets, of butter closing quiet and Pendragon being meant to win. This is not a symbol of commerce: commerce is a symbol of this.

In sketching this general and necessary

w*h*

attitude towards the art of Watts, particularly in the matter of allegory, I have taken deliberately these two very famous and obvious pictures, and I have occupied, equally deliberately, a considerable amount of space in expounding them. It is far better, in a subject so subtle and so bewildering as the relation between art and philosophy, that we should see how our conceptions and hypotheses really get on when applied systematically and at some length, to some perfectly familiar and existent object. A philosopher cannot talk about any single thing, down to a pumpkin, without showing whether he is wise or foolish; but he can easily talk about everything without anyone having any views about him beyond gloomy suspicions. But at this point I become fully conscious of another and most important kind of criticism, which has been and can be levelled against the allegories of Watts; and which must be, by the nature of things, evoked by the particular line of discussion or reflection that I have here adopted.

It may be admitted that Watts' art is not merely literary in the sense in which I have originally used the term It may be admitted that there is truth in the general position I have sketched out—that Watts is not a man copying literature or philosophy, but rather a man copying the great spiritual and central realities which literature and philosophy also set out to copy. It may be admitted that *Mammon* is obviously an attempt to portray, not a twopenny phrase, but a great idea. But along with all these admissions, it will certainly be said, by the most powerful and recent school in art criticism, that all this amounts to little more than a difference between a mean and a magnificent blunder. Pictorial art, it will be said, has no more business, as such, to portray great ideas than small ideas. Its affair is with its own technique, with the love of a great billowing line for its own sake, of a subtle and perfect tint for its own sake. If a man mistakes his trade and attends to the technique of another, the sublimity of his mind is only a very slight consolation. If I summon a paper-hanger to cover the walls, and he insists on playing the piano, it matters little whether he plays Beethoven or "The Yachmak." If I charter a pianist, and he is found drinking in the wine cellar, it matters little whether he has made his largest hole in good Burgundy or bad Marsala. If the whole of this question of great ideas and small ideas, of large atmospheres and superficial definitions, of the higher and the lower allegory, if all this be really irrelevant to the discussion of the position of a painter, then, indeed, we have been upon an idle track. As I think I shall show in a moment, this is a very inadequate view of the matter. But it does draw our attention to an aspect of the matter which must, without further delay, be discussed. That aspect, as I need hardly say, is the technique of Watts.

There is of course a certain tendency among all interesting and novel critical philosophers to talk as if they had discovered things which it is perfectly impossible that any human being could ever have denied; to shout that the birds fly, and declare that in spite of persecution they will still assert that cows have four legs. In this way some raw pseudo-scientists talk about heredity or the physical basis of life, as if it were not a thing embedded

DEATH CROWNING INNOCENCE

in every creed and legend, and even the very languages of men. In this way some of the new oligarchists of to-day imagine they are attacking the doctrine of human equality by pointing out that some men are stronger or cleverer than others; as if they really believed that Danton and Washington thought that every man was the same height and had the same brains. And something of this preliminary cloud of folly or misunderstanding attaches doubtless to the question of the technical view, that is the solely technical view, of painting. If the principle of "art for art's sake" means simply that there is a solely technical view of painting, and that it must be supreme on its own ground, it appears a piece of pure madness to suppose it other than true. Surely there never was really a man who held that a picture that was vile in colour and weak in drawing was a good picture because it was a picture of Florence Nightingale? Surely there never was really a man who said that when one leg in a drawing was longer than another, yet they were both the same length because the artist painted it for an altar piece! When the new critics, with

a burst of music and a rocket shower of epigrams enunciated their new criticism, they
must at any rate have meant something more
than this. Undoubtedly they did mean something more; they meant that a picture was
not a good vehicle for moral sentiment at all;
they meant that not only was it not the better
for having a philosophic meaning, but that it
was worse. This, if it be true, is beyond all
question a real indictment of Watts.

About the whole of this Watts controversy
about didactic art, there is at least one perfectly plain and preliminary thing to be said.
It is said that art cannot teach a lesson. This
is true, and the only proper addition is the
statement that neither, for the matter of that,
can morality teach a lesson. For a thing to
be didactic, in the strict and narrow and
scholastic sense, it must be something about
facts or the physical sciences: you can only
teach a lesson about such a thing as Euclid or
the making of paper boats. The thing is quite
inapplicable to the great needs of man, whether
moral or æsthetic. Nobody ever held a class
in philanthropy, with fifteen millionaires in
a row writing cheques. Nobody ever held

evening continuation classes in martyrdom, or drilled boys in a playground to die for their country. A picture cannot give a plain lesson in morals; neither can a sermon. A didactic poem was a thing known indeed among the ancients and the old Latin civilisation, but as a matter of fact it scarcely ever professed to teach people how to live the higher life. It taught people how to keep bees.

Since we find, therefore, that ethics is like art, a mystic and intuitional affair, the only question that remains is, have they any kinship. If they have not, a man is not a man, but two men and probably more: if they have, there is, to say the least of it, at any rate a reasonable possibility that a note in moral feeling might have affinity with a note in art, that a curve in law, so to speak, may repeat a curve in draughtsmanship, that there may be genuine and not artificial correspondences between a state of morals and an effect in painting. This would, I should tentatively suggest, appear to be a most reasonable hypothesis. It is not so much the fact that there is no such thing as allegorical art, but rather the fact that there is no art that is not allegorical.   But the meanings expressed in high and delicate art are not to be classed under cheap and external ethical formulæ, they deal with strange vices and stranger virtues. Art is only unmoral in so far as most morality is immoral.   Thus Mr Whistler when he drops a spark of perfect yellow or violet into some glooming pool of the nocturnal Thames is, in all probability, enunciating some sharp and wholesome moral comment.   When the young Impressionists paint dim corners of meadows or splashes of sunlight in the wood, this does not mean necessarily that they are unmoral; it may only mean that they are a very original and sincere race of stern young moralists.

Now if we adopt this general theory of the existence of genuine correspondences between art and moral beauty, of the existence, that is to say, of genuine allegories, it is perfectly clear whereir the test of such genuineness must consist.   It must consist in the nature of the technique.   If the technique, considered as technique, is calculated to evoke in us a certain kind of pleasure, and there is an analogous pleasure in the meaning considered

A STORY FROM BOCCACCIO

as meaning, then there is a true wedding of
the arts. But if the pleasure in the technique
be of a kind quite dissimilar in its own sphere,
to the pleasure in the spiritual suggestion,
then it is a mechanical and unlawful union, and
this philosophy, at any rate, forbids the banns.
If the intellectual conceptions uttered in
Michael Angelo's *Day of Judgment* in the
Sistine Chapel were the effect of a perfect and
faultless workmanship, but the workmanship
such as we should admire in a Gothic missal or
a picture by Gerard Dow, we should then say,
that absolute excellence in both departments
did not excuse their being joined. The thing
would have been a mere accident, or con-
venience. Just as two plotters might communi-
cate by means of a bar or two of music, so
these subtle harmonies of colour and form
would have been used for their detached
and private ends by the dark conspirators of
morality.

Now there is nothing in the world that is
really so thoroughly characteristic of Watts'
technique as the fact that it does almost
startlingly correspond to the structure of his
spiritual sense. If such pictures as *The Dweller*

in the Innermost and *Mammon* and *Diana and Endymion* and *Eve Repentant* had neither titles nor author, if no one had heard of Watts or heard of Eve; if, for the matter of that, the pictures had neither human nor animal form, it would be possible to guess something of the painter's attitude from the mere colour and line. If Watts painted an arabesque, it would be moral; if he designed a turkey carpet, it would be stoical. So individual is his handling that his very choice and scale of colours betrays him. A man with a keen sense of the spiritual and symbolic history of colours could guess at something about Watts from the mess on his palette. He would see giants and the sea and cold primeval dawns and brown earthmen and red earth-women lying in the heaps of greens and whites and reds, like forces in chaos before the first day of creation. A certain queer and yet very simple blue there is, for instance, which is like Titian's and yet not like it, which is more lustrous and yet not less opaque, and which manages to suggest the north rather than Titian's south, in spite of its intensity; which suggests also the beginning of things rather than their maturity;

LORD LYTTON

a hot spring of the earth rather than Titian's opulent summer. Then there is that tremendous autochthonous red, which was the colour of Adam, whose name was Red Earth. It is, if one may say so, the clay in which no one works, except Watts and the Eternal Potter. There are other colours that have this character, a character indescribable except by saying that they come from the palette of Creation —a green especially that reappears through portraits, allegories, landscapes, heroic designs, but always has the same fierce and elfish look, like a green that has a secret. It may be seen in the signet ring of Owen Meredith, and in the eyes of the *Dweller in the Innermost*. But all these colours have, as I say, the first and most characteristic and most obvious of the mental qualities of Watts; they are simple and like things just made by God. Nor is it, I think, altogether fanciful to push this analogy or harmony a step further and to see in the colours and the treatment of them the other side or typical trait which I have frequently mentioned as making up the identity of the painter. He is, as I say, a stoic; therefore to some extent, at least, a pagan; he has no special sympathy with Celtic intensity, with Catholic mysticism, with Romanticism, with all the things that deal with the cells of the soul, with agonies and dreams. And I think a broad distinction between the finest pagan and the finest Christian point of view may be found in such an approximate phrase as this, that paganism deals always with a light shining on things, Christianity with a light shining through them. That is why the whole Renascence colouring is opaque, the whole pre-Raphaelite colouring transparent. The very sky of Rubens is more solid than the rocks of Giotto : it is like a noble cliff of immemorial blue marble. The artists of the devout age seemed to regret that they could not make the light show through everything, as it shows through the little wood in the wonderful *Nativity* of Botticelli. And that is why, again, Christianity, which has been attacked so strangely as dull and austere, invented the thing which is more intoxicating than all the wines of the world, stained glass windows.

Now Watts, with all his marvellous spirituality, or rather because of his peculiar type of marvellous spirituality, has the Platonic, the

DAWN

philosophic, rather than the Catholic order of
mysticism.   And it can scarcely be a coinci-
dence that here again we feel it to be something that could almost be deduced from the
colours if they were splashed at random about
a canvas.   The colours are mystical, but they
are not transparent; that is, not transparent
in the very curious but unmistakable sense in
which the colours of Botticelli or Rossetti are
transparent.   What they are can only be described as iridescent.   A curious lustre or
glitter, conveyed chiefly by a singular and individual brush-work, lies over all his great
pictures.   It is the dawn of things: it is the
glow of the primal sense of wonder; it is
the sun of the childhood of the world; it is
the light that never was on sea or land; but
still it is a light shining on things, not shining
through them.   It is a light which exhibits and
does honour to this world, not a light that
breaks in upon this world to bring it terror or
comfort, like the light that suddenly peers
round the corner of some dark Gothic chapel
with its green or golden or blood-red eyes.
The Gothic artists, as I say, would have liked
men's bodies to become like burning glass (as

the figures in their windows do), that the light might pass through them. There is no fear of light passing through Watts' *Cain*.

These analogies must inevitably appear fantastic to those who do not accept the general hypothesis of a possible kinship between pictorial and moral harmonies in the psychology of men; but to those who do accept this not very extravagant hypothesis, it may, I think, be repeated by way of summary, that the purely technical question of Watts' colour scheme does provide us, at least suggestively, with these two parallels. Watts, so far as his moral and mental attitude can be expressed by any phrases of such brevity, has two main peculiarities: first, a large infantile poetry which delights in things fresh, raw and gigantic; second, a certain Greek restraint and agnostic severity, which throws a strong light on this world as it is. The colours he uses have also two main peculiarities: first, a fresh, raw and as it were, gigantic character; secondly, an opaque reflected light, unlike the mediæval lighting, a strong light thrown on this world as it is.

Similar lines of comparison, so far as they appear to possess any value, could, of course, be very easily pointed out in connection with the character of Watts' draughtsmanship. That his lines are simple and powerful, that both in strength and weakness they are candid and austere, that they are not Celtic, not Catholic, and not romantic lines of draughtsmanship, would, I think, appear sufficiently clearly to anyone who has any instinct for this mode of judgment at all. In the matter of line and composition, of course, the same general contention applies as in the case of colour. The curve of the bent figure of *Hope*, considered simply as a curve, half repeating as it does the upper curve of the globe, suggests a feeling, a sense of fear, of simplicity, of something which lies near to the nature of the idea itself, the idea which inspires the title of the picture. The splendid rushing whirlpool of curves which constitutes, as it were, the ellipse of the two figures in *Diana and Endymion* is a positive inspiration. It is, simply as a form for a picture, a mere scheme of lines, the very soul of Greece. It is simple; it is full and free; it follows great laws of harmony, but it follows them swiftly and at will; it is headlong, and yet at rest, like the solid arch of a waterfall. It is a rushing and passionate meeting of two superb human figures; and it is almost a mathematical harmony. Technically, at least, and as a matter of outlines, it is probably the artist's masterpiece.

Before we quit this second department of the temperament of Watts, as expressed in his line, mention must be made of what is beyond all question the most interesting and most supremely personal of all the elements in the painter's designs and draughtsmanship. That is, of course, his magnificent discovery of the artistic effect of the human back. The back is the most awful and mysterious thing in the universe: it is impossible to speak about it. It is the part of man that he knows nothing of; like an outlying province forgotten by an emperor. It is a common saying that anything may happen behind our backs: transcendentally considered the thing has an eerie truth about it. Eden may be behind our backs, or Fairyland. But this mystery of the human back has again its other side in the strange impression produced on those behind: to walk behind anyone along a lane is a thing that, properly speaking, touches the oldest nerve of

EVE REPENTANT

awe. Watts has realised this as no one in art or letters has realised it in the whole history of the world : it has made him great. There is one possible exception to his monopoly of this magnificent craze. Two thousand years before, in the dark scriptures of a nomad people, it had been said that their prophet saw the immense Creator of all things, but only saw Him from behind. I do not know whether even Watts would dare to paint that. But it reads like one of his pictures : like the most terrific of all his pictures, which he has kept veiled.

I need not instance the admirable and innumerable cases of this fine and individual effect. *Eve Repentant* (that fine picture), in which the agony of a gigantic womanhood is conveyed as it could not be conveyed by any power of visage, in the powerful contortion of the muscular and yet beautiful back—is the first that occurs to the mind. The sad and sardonic picture painted in later years, *For he had Great Possessions*—showing the young man of the Gospel loaded with his intolerable pomp of garments and his head sunken out of sight —is of course another. Others are slighter

instances, like *Good Luck to your Fishing*. He
has again carried the principle, in one instance,
to an extreme seldom adopted, I should fancy,
either by artist or man. He has painted a
very graceful portrait of his wife, in which that
lady's face is entirely omitted, the head being
abruptly turned away. But it is indeed idle to
multiply these instances of the painter's hobby
(if one may use the phrase) of the worship of
the human back, when all such instances have
been dwarfed and overshadowed by the one
famous and tremendous instance that everyone knows. *Love and Death* is truly a great
achievement: if it stood alone it would have
made a man great. And it fits in with a
peculiar importance with the general view I
am suggesting of the Watts technique. For
the whole picture really hangs, both technically and morally, upon one single line, a line
that could be drawn across a blank canvas, the
spine-line of the central figure of Death with
its great falling garment. The whole composition, the whole conception, and I was going to
say, the whole moral of the picture, could be
deduced from that single line. The moral of
the picture (if moral were the right phrase for

LOVE AND DEATH

these things,) is, it is scarcely necessary to point out, the monument of about as noble a silence and suppression as the human mind ever bent itself to in its pride. It is the great masterpiece of agnosticism. In that picture agnosticism, not the cheap and querulous incredulity which abuses the phrase, but loyal and consistent agnosticism, which is as willing to believe good as evil and to harbour faith as doubt, has here its great and pathetic place and symbol in the house of the arts. It is the artistic embodiment of reverent ignorance at its highest, fully as much as the Divine Comedy is the artistic embodiment of Christianity.

Technically, in a large number of cases, it is probably true that Watts' portraits, or some of them at least, are his most successful achievements. But here also we find our general conclusion: for if his portraits are his best pictures, it is certainly not because they are merely portraits; if they are in some cases better than his symbolic designs, it is certainly not because they are less symbolic. In his gallery of great men, indeed, we find Watts almost more himself than anywhere else. Most men are allegorical when they are painting allegories, but Watts is allegorical when he is painting an old alderman. A change passes over that excellent being, a change of a kind to which aldermen are insufficiently inured. He begins to resolve into the primal elements, to become dust and the shadow, to become the red clay of Adam and the wind of God. His eyes become, in spite of his earnest wish, the fixed stars in the sky of the spirit; his complexion begins to show, not the unmeaning red of portraits and miniatures, but that secret and living red which is within us, and which is the river of man. The astounding manner in which Watts has, in some cases, treated his sitters, is one of the most remarkable things about his character. He is not (it is almost absurd to have to mention such a thing about the almost austere old democrat) a man likely to flatter a sitter in any worldly or conventional sense. Nor is he, for the matter of that, a man likely to push compliments far from any motive: he is a strict, and I should infer, a candid man. The type of virtues he chiefly admires and practises, are the reverse of those which would encourage a courtier or even a universalist. But he scarcely ever paints a man without making him about five times as magnificent as he really looks. The real men appear, if they present themselves afterwards, like mean and unsympathetic sketches from the Watts original.

The fact is that this indescribable primalism, which we have noted as coming out in the designs, in the titles and in Watts' very oil-colours, is present in this matter in a most extraordinary way. Watts does not copy men at all: he makes them over again. He dips his hand in the clay of chaos and begins to model a man named William Morris or a man named Richard Burton: he is assisted, no doubt, in some degree by a quaint old text-book called Reality, with its stiff but suggestive woodcuts and its shrewd and simple old hints. But the most that can be said for the portraiture is, that Watts asks a hint to come and stop with him, puts the hint in a chair in his studio and stares at him. The thing that comes out at last upon the canvas is not generally a very precise picture of the sitter, though, of course, it is almost always a very accurate picture of the universe.

And yet while this, on the one side, is true enough, the portraits are portraits, and very fine portraits. But they are dominated by an element which is the antithesis of the whole tendency of modern art, that tendency which for want of a better word we have to call by the absurd name of optimism. It is not, of course, in reality a question of optimism in the least, but of an illimitable worship and wonder directed towards the fact of existence. There is a great deal of difference between the optimism which says that things are perfect and the optimism which merely says (with a more primeval modesty) that they are very good. One optimism says that a one-legged man has two legs because it would be so dreadful if he had not. The other optimism says that the fact that the one-legged was born of a woman, has a soul, has been in love and has stood alive under the stars, is a fact so enormous and thrilling that, in comparison, it does not matter whether he has one leg or five. One optimism says that this is the best of all possible worlds. The other says that it is certainly not the best of all possible worlds, but it is the best of all possible things that a world should be possible. Watts, as has been more than once more or less definitely suggested, is dominated

WILLIAM MORRIS

throughout by this prehistoric wonder. A man to him, especially a great man, is a thing to be painted as Fra Angelico painted angels, on his knees. He has indeed, like many brilliant men in the age that produced Carlyle and Ruskin, an overwhelming tendency to hero-worship. That worship had not, of course, in the case of these men any trace of that later and more denaturalised hero-worship, the tendency to worship madmen—to dream of vast crimes as one dreams of a love-affair, and to take the malformation of the soul to be the only originality. To the Carlylean (and Watts has been to some by no means inconsiderable extent a Carlylean), to the Carlylean the hero, the great man, was a man more human than humanity itself. In worshipping him you were worshipping humanity in a sacrament : and Watts seems to express in almost every line of his brush this ardent and reverent view of the great man. He overdoes it. Tennyson, fine as he was both physically and mentally, was not quite so much of a demi-god as Watts' splendid pictures would seem to suggest. Many other sitters have been subjected, past all recognition, to this kind of devout and

ethereal caricature. But the essential of the
whole matter was that the attitude of Watts
was one which might almost be called worship.
It was not, of course, that he always painted
men as handsome in the conventional sense,
or even as handsome as they were. William
Morris impressed most people as a very
handsome man : in Watts' marvellous portrait, so much is made of the sanguine face,
the bold stare, the almost volcanic suddenness
of the emergence of the head from the dark
green background, that the effect of ordinary
good looks, on which many of Morris's intimates
would probably have prided themselves, is in
some degree lost. Carlyle, again, when he
saw the painter's fine rendering of him, said
with characteristic surliness, that he "looked
like a mad labourer." Conventionally speaking,
it is of course, therefore, to be admitted that
the sitters did not always come off well. But
the exaggeration, or the distortion, if exaggeration or distortion there were, was always
effected in obedience to some almost awe-
struck notion of the greatness or goodness of the
great or good sitter. The point is not whether
Watts sometimes has painted men as ugly

DANTE GABRIEL ROSSETTI

as they were painted by the primary religious painters; the point is, as I have said, that he painted as they did, on his knees. Now no one thinks that Mr Sargent paints the Misses Wertheimer on his knees. His grimness and decision of drawing and colouring are not due to a sacred optimism. But those of Watts are due to this: are due to an intense conviction that there is within the sitter a great reality which has to give up its secret before he leaves the seat or the model's throne. Hence come the red violent face and minatory eyes of William Morris: the painter sought to express, and he did most successfully express, the main traits and meaning of Morris—the appearance of a certain plain masculine passion in the realm of decorative art. Morris was a man who wanted good wall-papers, not as a man wants a coin of the Emperor Constantine, which was the cloistered or abnormal way in which men had commonly devised such things: he wanted good wall-papers as a man wants beer. He clamoured for art: he brawled for it. He asserted the perfectly virile and ordinary character of the appetite for beauty. And he possessed and developed a power of moral violence on pure matters of taste which startled the flabby world of connoisseurship and opened a new era. He grew furious with furniture and denounced the union of wrong colours as men denounce an adultery. All this is expressed far more finely than in these clumsy sentences, in that living and leonine head in the National Portrait Gallery. It is exactly the same with Carlyle. Watts' Carlyle is immeasurably more subtle and true than the Carlyle of Millais, which simply represents him as a shaggy, handsome, magnificent old man. The uglier Carlyle of Watts has more of the truth about him, the strange combination of a score of sane and healthy visions and views, with something that was not sane, which bloodshot and embittered them all, the great tragedy of the union of a strong countryside mind and body with a disease of the vitals and something like a disease of the spirit. In fact, Watts painted Carlyle "like a mad labourer," because Carlyle was a mad labourer.

This general characteristic might of course be easily traced in all the portraits one by one. If space permitted, indeed such a process might be profitable ; for while we take careful

THOMAS CARLYLE

note of all the human triviality of faces, the one thing that we all tend to forget is that divine and common thing which Watts celebrates. It is the misfortune of the non-religious ages that they tend to cultivate a sense of individuality, not only at the expense of religion, but at the expense of humanity itself. For the modern portrait-painter not only does not see the image of God in his sitters, he does not even see the image of man. His object is not to insist on the glorious and solemn heritage which is common to Sir William Harcourt and Mr Albert Chevalier, to Count Tolstoy and Mr Wanklyn, that is the glorious and solemn heritage of a nose and two eyes and a mouth. The effort of the dashing modern is rather to make each of these features individual almost to the point of being incredible: it is his desire to paint the mouth whose grimace is inimitable, the eyes that could be only in one head, and the nose that never was on sea or land. There is value in this purely personal treatment, but something in it so constantly lost: the quality of the common humanity. The new art gallery is too like a museum of freaks, it is too

wild and wonderful, like a realistic novel.
Watts errs undoubtedly on the other side.
He makes all his portraits too classical. It
may seem like a paradox to say that he makes
them too human; but humanity is a *classis*
and therefore classical. He recurs too much
to the correct type which includes all men.
He has, for instance, a worship of great men
so complete that it makes him tend in the
direction of painting them all alike. There
may be too much of Browning in his Tennyson,
too much of Tennyson in his Browning.
There is certainly a touch of Manning in his
John Stuart Mill, and a touch of the Minotaur
in many of his portraits of Imperial politicians.
While he celebrates the individual with a
peculiar insight, it is nevertheless always
referred to a general human type. We feel
when we look at even the most extraordinary
of Watts' portraits, as for instance the portrait
of Lord Stratford de Redcliffe, that before
Lord Stratford de Redcliffe was born, and
apart from that fact, there was such a thing as
a human being. When we look at a brilliant
modern canvas like that of Mr Sargent's
portrait of Wertheimer, we do not feel that

any human being analogous to him had of
necessity existed. We feel that Mr Wertheimer might have been created before the
stars. Watts has a tendency to resume his
characters into his background as if they were
half returning to the forces of nature. In his
more successful portraits, the actual physical
characteristics of the sitter appear to be something of the nature of artistic creations; they
are decorative and belong to a whole. We
feel that he has filled in the fiery orange of
Swinburne's hair as one might fill in a gold
or copper panel. We know that he was
historically correct in making the hair orange,
but we cannot get rid of a haunting feeling
that if his scheme had been a little different
he would have made it green. This indescribable sentiment is particularly strong in the
case of the portrait of Rossetti. Rossetti is
dressed in a dark green coat which perfectly
expresses his sumptuous Pre-Raphaelite affectation. But we do not feel that Rossetti has
adopted the dark green coat to suit his dark
red beard. We rather feel that if anyone
had seized Rossetti and forcibly buttoned
him up in the dark green coat he would

have grown the red beard by sheer force
of will.

Before we quit the subject of portraiture a
word ought to be said about two exceedingly
noble portraits, those of Matthew Arnold and
Cardinal Manning. The former is interesting
because, as an able critic said somewhere (I
wish I could remember who he was or where
he wrote), this is the one instance of Watts
approaching tentatively a man whom he in all
reasonable probability did not understand.
In this particular case the picture is a hundred
times better for that. The portrait-painter of
Matthew Arnold obviously ought not to understand him, since he did not understand himself.
And the bewilderment which the artist felt
for those few hours, reproduced in a perfect,
almost in an immortal picture, the bewilderment which the sitter felt from the cradle to
the grave. The bewilderment of Matthew
Arnold was more noble and faithful than most
men's certainty, and Watts has not failed to
give that nobility a place even greater perhaps
than that which he would have given to it
had he been working on that fixed theory of
admiration in which he dealt with Tennyson

GOOD LUCK TO YOUR FISHING

w/

or Morris. The sad sea-blue eyes of Matthew
Arnold seemed to get near to the fundamental
sadness of blue. It is a certain eternal bleak-
ness in the colour which may for all I know
have given rise to the legend of blue devils.
There are times at any rate when the bluest
heavens appear only blue with those devils.
The portrait of Cardinal Manning is worth a
further and special notice, because it is an
illustration of the fact to which I have before
alluded: the fact that while Watts in one
sense always gets the best out of his sitters,
he does not by any means always get the
handsomest out of them. Manning was a
singularly fine-looking man, even in his emacia-
tion. A friend of mine, who was particularly
artistic both by instinct and habits, gazed for
a long time at a photograph of the terrible
old man clad in those Cardinal's robes and
regalia in which he exercised more than a
Cardinal's power, and said reflectively, "He
would have made his fortune as a model." A
great many of the photographs of Manning,
indeed almost any casual glimpses of him,
present him as more beautiful than he appears
in Watts' portrait. To the ordinary onlooker

there was behind the wreck of flesh and the splendid skeleton, the remains of a very handsome English gentleman; relics of one who might have hunted foxes and married an American heiress. Watts has no eyes for anything except that sublime vow which he would himself repudiate, that awful Church which he would himself disown. He exaggerates the devotionalism of Manning. He is more ascetic than the ascetics; more Catholic than Catholicism. Just so, he would be, if he were painting the Sheik-el-Islam, more Moslem than the Mahomedans. He has no eyes but for ideas.

Watts' allegories and Watts' portraits exhaust the subject of his art. It is true that he has on rare occasions attempted pictures merely reproducing the externals of the ordinary earth. It is characteristic of him that he should have once, for no apparent reason in particular, painted a picture of two cart-horses and a man. It is still more characteristic of him that this one picture of a trivial group in the street should be so huge as to dwarf many of his largest and most transcendental canvases; that the incidental harmless drayman should be more gigantic than the Prince of this World or Adam or the Angel of Death. He condescends to a detail and makes the detail more vast than a cosmic allegory. One picture, called "The First Oyster," he is reported to have painted in response to a challenge which accused him or his art of lacking altogether the element of humour. The charge is interesting, because it suggests a comparison with the similar charge commonly brought against Gladstone. In both charges there is an element of truth, though not complete truth. Watts proved no doubt that he was not wholly without humour by this admirable picture. Gladstone proved that he was not wholly without humour by his reply to Mr Chaplin, by his singing of "Doo-dah," and by his support of a grant to the Duke of Coburg. But both men were singularly little possessed by the mood or the idea of humour. To them had been in peculiar fulness revealed the one great truth which our modern thought does not know and which it may possibly perish through not knowing. They knew that to enjoy life means to take it seriously. There is an eternal kinship between solemnity and high spirits, and almost the very name of it is Gladstone. Its other name is Watts. They knew that not only life, but every detail of life, is most a pleasure when it is studied with the gloomiest intensity. They knew that the men who collect beetles are jollier than the men who kill them, and that the men who worshipped beetles (in ancient Egypt) were probably the jolliest of all. The startling cheerfulness of the old age of Gladstone, the startling cheerfulness of the old age of Watts, are both entirely redolent of this exuberant seriousness, this uproarious gravity. They were as happy as the birds, because like the birds, they were untainted by the disease of laughter. They are as awful and philosophical as children at play: indeed they remind us of a truth true for all of us, though capable of misunderstanding, that the great aim of a man's life is to get into his second childhood.

Of his work we have concluded our general survey. It has been hard in conducting such a survey to avoid the air of straying from the subject. But the greatest hardness of the subject is that we cannot stray from the subject. This man has attempted, whether he has succeeded or no, to paint such pictures of such things that no one shall be able to get outside them ; that everyone should be lost in them for ever, like wanderers in a mighty park. Whether we strike a match or win the Victoria Cross, we are still giants sprawling in Chaos. Whether we hide in a monastery or thunder on a platform, we are still standing in the Court of Death. If any experience at all is genuine, it affects the philosophy of these pictures ; if any halfpenny stamp supports them, they are the better pictures ; if any dead cat in a dust-bin contradicts them, they are the worse pictures. This is the great pathos and the great dignity of philosophy and theology. Men talk of philosophy and theology as if they were something specialistic and arid and academic. But philosophy and theology are not only the only democratic things, they are democratic to the point of being vulgar, to the point, I was going to say, of being rowdy. They alone admit all matters ; they alone lie open to all attacks. All other sciences may, while studying their own, laugh at the rag-tag and bob-tail of other sciences. An astronomer may sneer at animalculæ which are very like stars; an entomologist may scorn the stars, which are very like animalculæ. Physiologists may think it dirty to grub about in the grass; botanists may think it dirtier to grub about in an animal's inside. But there is nothing that is not relevant to these more ancient studies. There is no detail, from buttons to kangaroos, that does not enter into the gay confusion of philosophy. There is no fact of life, from the death of a donkey to the General Post Office, which has not its place to dance and sing in, in the glorious Carnival of theology.

Therefore I make no apology if I have asked the reader, in the course of these remarks, to think about things in general. It is not I, but George Frederick Watts, who asks the reader to think about things in general. If he has not done this he has failed. If he has not started in us such trains of reflection as I am now concluding and many more and many better, he has failed. And this brings me to my last word. Now and again Watts has failed. I am afraid that it may possibly be inferred from the magniloquent language which I have frequently, and with a full consciousness of my act, applied to this great man, that I think the whole of his work technically triumphant. Clearly it is not. For I believe that often he has scarcely known what he is doing; I believe that he has been in the dark when the lines came wrong; that he has been still deeper in the dark and things came right. As I have already pointed out, the vague lines which his mere physical instinct would make him draw, have in them the curves of the Cosmos. His automatic manual action is, I think, certainly a revelation to others, certainly a revelation to himself. Standing before a dark canvas upon some quiet evening, he has made lines and something has happened. In such an hour the strange and splendid phrase of the Psalm he has literally fulfilled. He has gone on because of the word of meekness and truth and of righteousness. And his right hand has taught him terrible things.

INDEX

(The titles of Pictures are printed in italics)

INDEX

INDEX

173

INDEX

Rossetti, 39, 133; with Sargent, 153; with Whistler, 14, 17; the essential spirit of his work, 24-30; his love of robustness, 29; his art eminently public, 51-54; his idealism like Milton's, 30; his optimism, 146; his theory and practice of portrait-painting, 77, 78, 143-154; his technique generally, 116, 119, 125, 126; his colour, 126-129, 133, 134; his draughtsmanship, 28, 29, 135; his composition and line, 135, 136.

Whistler, 13, 14, 17, 40, 41, 122.

Wounded Heron, The, 46, 47.

Yeats, W. B., his Celticism, 24, 28.

THE
POPULAR LIBRARY OF ART